Sex, Love, and Other Emotions

Sarai W. and Just Duléa

Conviction 2 Change LLC
www.conviction2change.com

Sex, Love, and Other Emotions

Edition 2018

Copyright © 2018 Sarai Waters, Taylor D. Duckett

All Rights Reserved

This book and parts thereof may not be reproduced in any form, stored in a retrieval system, or transmitted in any form by any means (electronic, mechanical, photocopy, recording, or otherwise) without prior written permission from the author and publisher, except as provided by the United States of America copyright law.

Published by Conviction 2 Change LLC
www.conviction2change.com

Library Congress Control Number: 2018904599
ISBN: 0692210238
ISBN-13: 978-0-692-10823-9

Cover Design: Kayla Lott
Editor: Taylor D. Duckett

Dedication

To God, for keeping us sane through the process; You're the real M.V.P.!

To those who have been through the wringer but have decided to love again, to those becoming whole, and to the men that inspired us.

Table of Contents

1.	Caught	1
2.	I'm Coming Soon	2
3.	I Knew You	3
4.	Connected	4
5.	A Different Type of Attraction	4
6.	One Night	5
7.	Voiceless	6
8.	Are you Ready?	7
9.	Let Me Count the Ways	8
10.	Yours Truly	9
11.	An Issue of Time	10
12.	Forfeit	10
13.	Someone That I Used to Know	11
14.	Homeboy Next Door	12
15.	I Saw Myself	13
16.	Counting 2.0	14
17.	Feelings	16
18.	Awakening	17
19.	Melting	18
20.	Perfect Fit	19
21.	Losing Control	20
22.	Passing Ships	20
23.	In and Out of Time	21
24.	Boaz and Ruth	22
25.	Cloaked and Innocence	23
26.	First Kiss	24
27.	You Love Me	24
28.	Sex	25
29.	Taboo	26
30.	Sex in Church	27
31.	First Time	29

32.	Twice the Blushing Virgin	30
33.	Wait for It	31
34.	Don't Awaken	31
35.	Inferno	32
36.	Canvas	33
37.	My Love, The Sun	34
38.	What I Want to Do with You	35
39.	The Five Senses	36
40.	Breakfast	38
41.	A Need to Love You	39
42.	Desire	40
43.	Dearly Beloved	42
44.	Tease	43
45.	Rock Around the Clock	44
46.	To You	46
47.	Thirsty	46
48.	Genuine	47
49.	What Do You See?	49
50.	You Don't See Me	49
51.	Shoot Straight	50
52.	Disarmed	51
53.	Mírame	52
54.	Show Me	53
55.	Getting it Right	54
56.	I Stepped Back	54
57.	The Shift	55
58.	This Is New	56
59.	A Rib Out of Place	57
60.	30 Minutes	58
61.	The Sound of My Thoughts	59
62.	Longing	59
63.	Sunrise	60
64.	What I Miss Most	61

65.	Sacrifices	62
66.	Five W's	63
67.	The Beginning of the End	64
68.	Unsteady	65
69.	Rest	66
70.	Broken(ness)	67
71.	Hearts Don't Break	68
72.	Love Hurts	68
73.	Twice the Fool	69
74.	Letting Go	70
75.	Old Friend	71
76.	Good News	72
77.	Friend Zone	73
78.	How to Be Just Friends	74
79.	It's Complicated	74
80.	For Free? (Nigga Please!)	75
81.	Situationship	77
82.	I Gave You Agape	78
83.	X Factor	79
84.	Possibilities	80
85.	As It Was in the Beginning	81
86.	The Waiting	82
87.	Until Next Time	83
88.	I Know	84
89.	Redeemed	85
90.	Fear	86
91.	Love TKO	87
92.	I Will Pray for You	88
93.	Trauma	89
94.	Settling	89
95.	Choices	90

96.	Denial	90
97.	A Heart Under Construction	91
98.	Decidedly Whole	92
99.	Love You	93
100.	I Used to Love to Hate Her	94
101.	Fortress	95
102.	Reclaiming	96
103.	Healing	97
104.	Freedom	98
105.	A Letter to My Ex	99
106.	Love and Lost	100
107.	I Forgive You	101
108.	Scars	102
109.	To Those Who Hurt	103

About the Author – Sarai W.

About the Author – Just Duléa

Sex…
    The subject of my dreams that eludes reality

Love…
    Eros, agape, trading one for the other, still empty of both

Other Emotions …
    The miscellany of life that when ignored…EXPLODES!

Caught

I made a mistake today.
I got caught up in my feelings and almost got stuck.
We give our emotions too much power over us.
Not that we should ignore them,
But we shouldn't allow them to run wild.
If I could choose to have only three,
I would choose joy, love, and hope.
Every other one could go.
Just know, that since we are owners of a complete emotional range,
Let's make sure to use them wisely.
If you ever get caught in your feelings
Just make sure you don't get stuck.

I'm Coming Soon

"I'm coming soon."

Words that sent a chill down my spine
A shiver through my body.
My stomach turned into a top-notch gymnast,
Doing a multitude of fast paced backflips.
My heart became a bunch of butterflies flying every which way.
All because you said,

"I'm coming soon."

I welcome you.
Until you get here,
I'll wait for you.
I just pray that I'm ready for you.

I Knew You

I saw you. How could I miss you? You were standing there, unassuming yet beautiful. Masculine yet sensitive.

You spoke, I stared and had to look away and catch myself. I was nervous because I felt you look at me. You saw me, beyond the natural. You investigated my spirit, you saw me. I loved it, but it made me uneasy.

I was uneasy because I felt it, I felt the pull. The pull I felt so many times before. You saw me and when I looked at you, I saw you too. I saw your spirit and I liked it. When I looked at you, so much I saw the reflection of God, the image of God in you, that someone had to remind me that you were beautiful physically too.

We spoke. We spoke about simple things, the basics yet I felt deep down that I knew you. I knew you and I loved you from that moment. My spirit knew what my head was trying to deny and what it hadn't been able to perceive yet. I knew that you were my Adam and I was your Eve.

You watched me, I watched you watch me. We played tag. You would steal a glance at me and I at you. Discretely of course because it was new, it was ours, for us alone.

It was time to go and I was sad because I missed you even though you were still there. Then we hugged and then I knew. There was a fire that turned my spirit upside down. It was different. Passionate but strong, cloaked in wisdom and the fear of God. A fire protected by holiness; it was wonderful. I knew yet, I did not know. My spirit was in another dimension and my head was struggling to keep up.

You left, and I missed you. I could not reason why I missed you we just met but I loved you. My logic and reasoning were shut down because I saw the God in you and knew you.

As you left, my spirit cried out. I couldn't say it aloud, not yet, I love you.

Connected

It's amazing how connected we are regardless the distance. That's how I know that our foundation is spiritual with things that will manifest in the natural as time goes on. God is real, and so is the love I feel for you.

A Different Type of Attraction

Most often when we think of attraction, we think of the physical or sexual.
Today I have seen the strongest attraction there is, spiritual.
When you find someone, who can see into your spirit and walk with you towards purpose
Keep them around.
The physical will fade, and sexual desire may wane
But the spirit will always remain.

One Night

It was *one night*
One night was all it took to get caught up
I let my guard down for a "gentleman"
A man who was gentle until I began telling him no

No, he didn't force me
I got nervous, let my guard down, and invited him in
I opened the door
Because I cared more about not hurting him than protecting me

I didn't let him go all the way
But he got close
Too close
We went way too far

I let him sweet talk and seduce me
I fell for it because I thought he cared
Besides, I thought I was strong
Strong enough to play with fire and not get burnt

No one can resist temptation in their own strength
No matter how super saved you think you are
Don't play with fire
Resist the temptation and run

I had a chance to run
God gave me an out
I almost didn't take it
Until it was too late

It's strange, leading up to that night we spoke often
Now he speaks through silence
I gave him more than he deserved
He left me with questions

The questions
The emotional, physical, and spiritual fatigue
All because I could not wait
I just had to have that *one night*; It wasn't worth it

Voiceless

When I chose protecting your ego, over protecting my body, I silenced myself. I was ashamed to admit, that I cared so little about myself, that I was willing to take anything. Knowing that it was bad for me but not caring. I almost walked away from God for you, just to have someone in my life. Never again, no one is worth my purpose.

Are You Ready?

Sex, this wonderful, transcendent experience,
A gift from God,
Is a physical expression of a spiritual union.

Are you ready?

Just because your body says yes,
Doesn't mean that you are ready.
It just means,
Your hormones work.

Condoms,
Pills,
Plan B,
Don't protect against everything.

Do you know the demon you're about to sleep with?

Sexually transmitted demons are a thing.
An improper soul tie can leave you feeling soulless.

Ever wonder why,
You keep going around and around with the same low down
Manifesting in a different body?
Spirit recognizes spirit.

It may be time for a STD check.

Let Me Count the Ways

1. He likes my name
2. He isn't afraid to stand up for what he believes in
3. He loves to travel
4. He is an amazing director and photographer
5. He's an apostle
6. He is unapologetically himself
7. He makes me laugh effortlessly
8. He gives me joy
9. He is the promise *(or so I thought…)*
10. He will take care of me
11. He's older and taller
12. He plays an instrument
13. He gets my weird
14. He's weird
15. He respects me and my time
16. One of the hardest working men I know
17. He knows how and when to apologize
18. He's a romantic and a sweetheart
19. He doesn't know personal space
20. He reminds me of my father (good qualities) and brother
21. He respects my input and faith-based decisions
22. His beautiful brown eyes
23. His passion and drive
24. He's a great friend
25. He's generous with his food, money, and time
26. My mom loves him
27. He has soft leg and facial hairs #beardgang
28. His laugh is contagious
29. He works out
30. Loves skateboarding and boxing
31. His fingers interlock with mine every time they meet
32. He's decisive
33. His accent

Yours Truly

I wish to speak of the on goings inside me. A place where, to be frank, I'd like you to take residency. Poetic essence sometimes fails me so allow me to paint a moving picture for you.

I see you and me sitting casually intertwined on a couch. A root beer in my hand and IPA in yours. I'd love to feel your lips pressed against mine the way you wrap yours around the bottle but forgive me. I'm being a bit forward, but I'd be cool if you leaned forward and put the bottle down, took mine, and proceeded to press me into the couch. Squish me if you will, I'm strong enough to bear the weight of you.

The only issue now is the presence of clothes. That's easily resolved as everything I'm in is loose and stretchy. I planned an evening like this and played it out in my head, but this is only the beginning. Don't pay attention to the trembling or shallowness of breath because it just means you're doing something right.

I hope you're okay if I tell you to slow down or move a little to the left. I'm no expert, but I'm sure that I'll know when the time comes, and you'll know you've done your job when I do. Didn't know my thoughts would allow me to delve as deep as I wish you to go but hey, I had to grow up sometime.

Lie with me if you dare. I'll be yours truly. Yours forever and all you have to do is say yes, I'll undress you and our instincts will take care of the rest. Until then, this root beer tastes almost as good as I imagine you do.

An Issue of Time

We're not star crossed yet we're galaxies away.
We suffer from an affliction of time.
Time sets free yet also constructs and complicates.
Never able to synchronize
It was always too early for one of us.
Now, it's too late.
The time has passed.
There is no rewind, no resetting of the clock.
Now we walk away from one another
Remembering time shared
Lamenting time lost
All because we couldn't synchronize.

Forfeit

Forfeit: *To step back, renounce, give up, be disqualified.*

Et tu?
I thought that you were a match made in Heaven,
But maybe my dreams of you were just an alternate reality playing out.
Because it was never true.
I cared for you more than you cared for me.
I see it now, clearly.
So now, I bid you adieu.

Someone That I Used to Know

It didn't have to be this way. We could have been great together. But I changed, I said yes to God and His purposes. You didn't, you stayed the same and chose to conform. We drifted apart, and you spoke through silence. It was deafening. You left me on hold mid conversation and never returned to the phone. Leaving me wondering, until I realized that you had moved on and found another. Never saying a word, or letting me know, that the feelings weren't mutual.

Now I see you and while I loved you, I can't bear to know you. To look at you pains me. I once loved you, had things been different, we could have maybe even remained friends. Now, we're nothing at all. You're just someone that I used to know.

Homeboy Next Door

You're not the one I thought I wanted
But you're the one I didn't know I needed.
See, you saw me at my lowest but
You got me.
I saw you at your lowest but admired your hustle.
Your ability to see beyond the bullshit.
You have a personality of fire while mine is like ice.
I expected us to clash,
But we didn't.
You're like the homeboy next door
But will it become something more?

I Saw Myself

Tonight showed me that you are my other half.
I am the rib that you're missing.
You're the man I was designed to help and do life with.
We are so similar it's crazy.
We have similar taste and opinions on life.
When we get nervous, we fidget similarly.
We even ponder and process alike...
It's crazy!
I have never seen myself in anyone as much as I see myself in you.
It scares me a little but excites me too.
Just when I thought I was destined to be alone,
God sent you.

I wonder if you knew, that I saw myself in you and when I did it set off warning bells. But all I heard were wedding bells. When I saw myself in you, I should have run sooner than I did. It's God that I should have been excited to see. Instead, I was content with potentially settling for a "man" that I would have to raise. You couldn't lead me down the street, let alone in life. I knew that but thought you would step up to the challenge. I was wrong. When the sirens first sounded, I should have listened. At least I eventually admitted what I already knew, the man for me, wasn't you.

Counting 2.0

1. He's a sweetheart
2. He is openly affectionate
3. His hands are the hands of a hard worker
4. His touch is gentle
5. His calm demeanor instantly deflates any residual anger I may have toward him
6. His passion
7. His courage to endure his process
8. He is wonderfully direct. It's so refreshing
9. When he kisses me, I get weak!
10. He's bilingual and is teaching me
11. He's patient with me even though he has little patience elsewhere
12. His connection and love of family
13. He constantly professes his love for me
14. His hair is heavenly
15. He smells amazing
16. He's fucking adorable when he sleeps
17. He's athletic
18. He wants to go to Jerusalem
19. He tastes amazing lol
20. His height doesn't faze me
21. His age doesn't faze me
22. He asks me what I'm thinking and causes me to be painfully honest
23. He isn't afraid of p.d.a. and is causing me to come out of my comfort zone
24. He has integrity
25. He realizes that we are each other's reward.
26. The way he kisses my neck
27. And my face

28. And shoulder (I may have mentioned this one before. Oh well!)
29. I love how he isn't afraid to tell me how he feels about me. What he is thinking at that very moment.
30. I love how being in his presence makes me want to confess my love for him.
31. His skin is multicolored. It's beautiful!
32. He pays hella close attention to me and my habits
33. His straightforward attitude
34. He fusses over me to eat
35. He appreciates my poetry and singing
36. He's stubborn a.f.
37. Knows the value of hard work
38. His face it's almost as expressive as mine lol.
39. He enjoys reading

This was before he changed into the neglectful and indecisive man who isn't mature enough to know when to ask forgiveness. Or maybe he was the same man the whole time…

Feelings

Feelings, something I am very familiar with regarding impatience, frustration and fear, but this...this feeling you give me... I haven't well acquainted myself with. I feel too deeply when I think of you and it scares me.

I see your face in my mind's eye and the depths of my soul cry out for your touch. For your eyes to caress my frame and your lips to caress my lips while hands and hips graze hips.

Scatter brain thinking is all I'm good for when you're around. I feel like I can't breathe when you're near, and yet I'm suffocating while you're away.

Who would've thought I'd get you. This beautiful man with your grandeur and visions of greatness. You teach me and make me question things I thought I knew about you. I want to know more. Questions ranging from: What's your favor color to where's your spot? Can I play connect the dots with the beauty marks on your body as I learn your anatomy...?

Have I spoken too frankly again? Sorry. Like I said before, you make me feel deeply and I don't think these feelings are going away. They simply travel from one region of my body to the other.

I'm exhausted from building walls, and I just wanna take a break. Help me. Take the tools away and take my hand. Lead me. I'll follow.

That's all...for now.

Awakening

You have caused an awakening
At your touch ice thaws, blood runs through my veins again,
Life stirs.
I feel again
All blockages gone
My walls torn down and carted away
The only thing surrounding me
Is you
Drawing me into a place
Where love is shown before being spoken
As we enjoy each other
Knowing that we are the others reward.

Melting

Is this love that I'm feeling? The thing that warms my heart thawing out a heart that was encased

                              in

                                      ice?

You, you did this!

You helped me to feel and I both thank you and dismay because of it since now I feel things I have never felt before and it's…intense. Every feeling with you is as though it's brand new. It's like I am experiencing the world for the first time.

Was I even living before I met you? I'm honestly not sure.
If I was it was a lesser existence that I hope to never return to. I melt every time I'm around you.

I love and loathe every minute of it.

Perfect Fit

Love comes slowly and all at once.
I never used to believe this
Emotions, especially love, were immediately dismissed
I refused to let myself be swept off my feet least I fall
Worried that no one would be there to catch me if I did
Any time I felt love awaken
I subdued it as though my feelings were my enemy
Making my heart so cold
The arctic seemed blazing
But then I met you
Now I'm spiraling, quickly unraveling, losing control
I'm looking for the breaks but we're moving full speed ahead
I'm drowning in a sea of emotions
I didn't know existed
But you reached down and lent a helping hand
In that moment I knew
That we were a perfect fit
Everything about us works
I couldn't ask for anything more.

Losing Control

You just don't understand; I'm falling for you and I'm trying to catch myself. Not because you're not worth being liked, believe me you are. You're the last of a dying breed.

My mind is in a tug of war with my heart; one telling me to draw back, the other suggesting that I go all in. It's sense versus sensibility. I'm trying to hide how quickly I'm falling for you. I don't want to get hurt, I don't want to hurt you. Somehow, I know that no matter what, you'll be there.

I'm losing control. My walls are crashing down around me. Every time you're near, I find myself smiling more. I can't help it around you. You bring out a joy and happiness I didn't know was there. Buried so long under pain and past hurts but in a short time you've unearthed it, doing what no one else could.

I can't help the attraction. I don't want to help it. I'm losing control but with you I know it's going to be alright.

My walls were nothing more than a drawbridge.
You, a ship passing through.

Passing Ships

Like two ships passing in the night
Functioning similarly yet with unique designs
Acknowledging each other yet unaware
That the other holds their missing piece

In and Out of Time

She waited for him; he didn't know he was looking for her.
Until he found her; in that moment he saw her for the very first time.

From the time they first met she wondered, "who is he?"
Not wanting to be exposed before her other half, because she didn't know him yet.

From the time they first met, he felt something towards her, but didn't know what or why.
He stayed as close as reasonable for a time, until the right time.

From the time they first met they danced, in and out of time and each other's presence.
Watching as Chronos passed and gave way to Kairos.

In and out of time they moved, orbiting one another like the moon Earth, and the planets the Sun.
But never quite meeting, though they always knew the other was there.

Until the day that the clock struck Kairos; time linear and time eternal intersected.
The two individuals taking center stage; their love evident without words.

An attraction so strong they were pulled into each other's orbit, throwing the cosmos into chaos.
Throwing old systems out of sync as they became one.

> Now, they're timeless.
> And step together in and out of time.

Boaz and Ruth

You are Boaz and I am Ruth
You saw me moving in purpose and were enamored by me
I saw your gentle kindness and I felt safe
You saw my heart to serve and were blessed by it
I saw your love and felt secure

Thank you for stepping into purpose
For being a redeeming kinsman
Graciously filling a void left by another
A purpose abdicated
Even before I was yours you took care of me, thank you

It is you I want
You are like no other
With you I will always be fulfilled
Each day a new adventure
Let's do life together and birth a legacy

You are Boaz and I am Ruth
Together we will change the world.

Cloaked in Innocence

The innocence of God surrounds you.
Those who have eyes and discernment can see it.
Can see the purity.
The beauty of holiness.
The wonder of two people not afraid to be processed together
So that they never have to be apart.

There is purpose that surrounds you.
As you teach one another and learn God together.
As covenants are made, founded in love.
Secured by the peace of God.
Hidden by His mercy from those who seek to do harm.

There is joy that radiates from you.
The fruits of the Spirit abound in your garden.
As you retreat into a secret place where no one and nothing else matters.
Time stands still for you
Even when you get lost in the moment.
Each passing moment a small slice of eternity that has been brought into the now for your pleasure.

Take care young lovers
To enjoy the reward that God has set before you.
He has awakened love in you
For such a time as this.

First Kiss

The first kiss was an apology; the rest, a conversation making up for lost time.

You Love Me

You said to me three words I was longing to hear and wondered if I would ever. *"I love you"* sandwiched in between other statements to see if I would notice. I did, and you have no idea what it did to me. I was afraid that I would never be loved.

Not the way I desired to be, and that my affection would go unanswered. I braced myself for the rejection that I was just certain was going to come.

But it didn't.

Instead your words hung in the air surrounding me with a warmth that I usually only find in your arms. You love me, and I love you too. No longer am I afraid of what it's doing to me. And I see now that you aren't either.

Sex

My thoughts lately are dripping

                sex,

                          oozing

                                    innuendo.

Quite indecent really…
Or is it natural and I've just been taught otherwise?

When you look my way,
I can't quite explain the fire that starts in my spirit
and overtakes my soul.
It's an inferno of feelings,
some to be mentioned others to be displayed.

I can't get you out of my mind or my spirit.
and I must admit that I desire your body.
But I never say any of this.
Nor do I show it.

Instead
I pretend it's a dream what I feel,
while knowing that it's anything but.

Taboo

Done under the cover of darkness
Swept under the rug
Clandestine
Never spoken about above a whisper
Especially by those who consider themselves *"holy"*

Yet in the depths of the night
Thoughts of sexual escapades come

What do you do when you feel things so deeply
So vividly
That you wonder if it's really a dream

You wake up with a sense of shame
Because in your dreams you were happily screaming someone's name

You don't always pray away what you feel
If you do
Your repentance is halfhearted
Because you liked it
But are afraid to admit it

What do you do then?

> *We place taboos on things that need to be discussed*
> *Openly*

> *Darkness produces a harvest of shame*
> *Choking out the light that's waiting for you*
> *Once you're honest*
> *About your thorns*

> *One cannot bind*
> *What they're in bondage to*

Sex in Church

"What do you know about sex?
Absolutely nothing!
"Why?"
Because I grew up in the church…you can't talk about sex there.

As soon as you even *think* the word sex
You are pushed towards the nearest deliverance line,
Doused with oil,
Having hands laid on you, smacking you upside the head
Until you do a mercy, "fall out under the presence," to make it stop.

See, we all have questions about sex
But growing up in the church makes that topic
Taboo.

"Why?"

Probably because sex was designed to be pleasurable… so I've heard… and pleasure is forbidden in the church it seems.
The Lord promises joy but the church has put a ban on it like,
"Woah there, you're enjoying the things of God a little too much, you better chill out!"

Yet the church gets mad when people turn to worldly methods to get their answers.
That's how people get addicted to porn you know…

Anyway, people have questions about sex.
We are humans, thoughts happen, but I tell you this,
Don't ask your questions in church.
'Cause unless your pastor or priest is walking around with a renewed mind,
Hip to the fact that sex education is just as important as tithing,

Their response may be, *"wait on the Lord to reveal it to you."*

Well…I'm waiting on the Lord,
Not awakening love before it's time.
It does say to taste, and see that the Lord is good…
I'm starting to get a little bit hungry.
But in my mid – twenties, what I know about sex is absolutely nothing.
I have questions,
I just can't ask them in church.

First Time

I'm imagining an event that has yet to occur
But seems so real in my mind's eye
I imagine running my hands the length of your torso
Exploring everything
Lovers have no secrets
I can feel the passion of your kisses
Gentle while demanding more
Though you kiss my lips
It's felt everywhere
There's no part of me that isn't made alive by you
Then there's the moment we come one flesh…
Maybe I'm romanticizing this
Maybe not
Only time will tell

Time told.
It was sex
But I wanted to make love.
I thought they were the same.
They differ by one word
Intimacy.

Twice the Blushing Virgin

Is it possible to rewind the hands of time?
To go back to before a seal was broken,
Before the perimeter was breached
To become the blushing virgin once more
The color taking over your face once from fear
Is now from feeling all the right things
And knowing that your partner feels the same
Many say no,
No do overs.
I disagree,
It's happened to me.

Inner healing can heal those
Who want to be whole
And who are not afraid
To face those things
They have hidden from themselves.

Wait for It

All my life I've waited for it
To understand what all those love songs were about
To feel the passion that oozes out of Neo-Soul and R&B
The time has come and now,
I can't wait for it
I can't wait for all of the first we'll share
Our first date, first kiss, first time
Though every time will feel like the first with you
I've waited for it and I'm still waiting for it
But hopefully the wait is soon over.

Don't Awaken

Don't awaken R&B before its time.
You know,
Those songs that give you fever and leave you fiending for seconds
of pleasure
Having you say yes, opening your heart, and undressing your soul
in front of the wrong one
Trying to please a person giving them whatever they want, when all
they've provided you is grief.
Losing control because lust has taken over and called itself love
It isn't love, you just feel this way because it seems to never rain.
Thinking that they are the truth, but can you see God in them?
When all they want to do is a little something something but
there's no ascension.
Don't awaken R&B before its time.
Guard your playlists, from out of it flows the beginning of trouble.

Inferno

My mind is consumed with thoughts of you.
Every time you get near me it sets my spirit on fire
Because it recognizes you and the purpose in you.
Fever doesn't describe what and how you make me feel.
It's an inferno.
Burning deeply, pulsating and radiating to every part of me.
It's fire.
It's ice.
It's desire.
It's a whirlwind.
It's ecstasy and passion.
It's oblivion.
It's you & me.
Two fiery people burning brightly with and for each other.

Canvas

Your body is like a canvas I want to paint as you color mine.
                        We'll take it

                              S
                              L
                              O
                              W

                        and easy

Using deliberate and methodical *strokes*
                                      Lightly going over *every* inch
                  Leaving nothing blank or unexplored

Delicately changing techniques as we strive to create a masterpiece

                       No shadows or shades,
                           just light

Every time the brush hits the canvas
                                        It's an explosion of color
                  We're creating hues never seen

The depths of artistic expression we reach are beyond imagination

                  Before time, in time, and after time
                      Our art is boundless

                            Come
                        Create with me.

My Love, The Sun

You my love are like the sun shining brightly like the twinkle in your eye.

Do you believe in love at first sight?
Or is everything a matter of circumstance?

I believe in fate and first instincts,
Instincts as strong as gravity pulling us together,
Whispering that maybe there is something there
Be it a moment or an eternity to be shared.

I believe in order, yet I succumb to the chaos of emotion
Pulling in every direction demanding to be felt and lived.
Passion overflowing like the river banks on a summer day
Allowing those willing to let go to be swept away in its currents.

You're my sun providing the warmth I feel when you're near me as you light up life.

What I Want to Do with You

Oh, the things I want to do with you,
and for you.
Oh, the places I'll let you go...when the time comes.

You, me, 23?
Rocking all night, not stopping till we get enough.
I want to feel you everywhere as you feel me.
One hand up and around my thighs inducing sweet sighs,
The other hand resting on my breasts while your mouth and tongue are intertwined with mine.
All the while my hands drift slowly around your body, getting to know you better.
Ensuring I have your full attention.

I'm looking forward to setting a high score and going the distance.
I want us to wear ourselves out in the best way.
I want you.
I want your body on and tangled up in mine.
Creating new languages.
Let's get lost in one another while I let you in.
Leaving nothing untouched.

> *Oh, how active the imagination*
> *of the sexually frustrated.*
> *burning with a desire they cannot fill by any means,*
> *so instead it plays out in their dreams.*

> *Dreams, showcasing desires*
> *for one who is not The One.*

> *Upon waking,*
> *salvation questioned,*
> *repentance the first order of the day.*

The Five Senses

Heaven,
Sweet innocence,
Feigned shyness,
Dulce De Leche,
Fried chicken,
Turkey and lightly salted onions,
The best thing I've ever had…
That's what you taste like.

Cologne,
A breath of fresh air,
Love,
Sex,
Other drugs I'll never try…
That's what you smell like.

Laundry fresh out the dryer,
A teddy bear,
Strength,
Tenderness,
Static electricity,
Kinetic energy,
Love…
That's what you feel like.

Authority,
Integrity,
Music,
Gentle rain,
Love…
That's what you sound like.

Sexy,
Adorable,
Distinguished,
Beautifully shaded with multiple hues of melanin,
Everything that I could have ever thought ask to ask for,
More than I could have ever dreamed of,
My love,
My heart,
Mine…
That's what you look like.

God knows I love you for reasons I have yet discovered, but I look forward to learning everything there is to know about you every day I get to spend time with you as your lady.

I love you. You've broken my walls and the debris lay around me while I try to pick up the shattered and tattered pieces. But there's no point because I'll never recover these walls, and I don't want to.

You're worth transparency and vulnerability. I hope you understand the weight of what I'm saying. I hope to be the first and last…but that's a discussion for another day.

Breakfast

Forever inspiring life changing experiences with you

Stolen glances/ Kisses/ Near misses/ Hand holding/ Foot coddling

I've missed this, us.
We're great together.
I see it, I know you do too,
this undeniable chemistry that beckons one to another.

I love you.

I wish I could string together the phrase
and hang it around your neck
So you'll never forget.
Never doubt my love for you,
not even for a moment.

Be mine.

We could live in the moments between bites of
cream cheese bagels and syrupy waffles
I'll be all the vanilla caffeine you need
You'll be my caramel delight.

I love you.
I can't say it enough,
But I'll try as long as you're listening, my love.

Te amo…

    I've never enjoyed breakfast as much as I did on those mornings with you.

A Need to Love You

What is this word "need" doing in my vocabulary when it comes to you? I see you in the distance and I can't help feeling like I need you near me. Me, who valued my separation and alone time. I find myself thinking silly thoughts that follow the lines of missing you. All roads lead back to you.

I speak the words *"I love you"* so effortlessly because you make it so easy to love you. You walk in my line of sight and I automatically feel drawn to you. I want your hand in mine and your face in my neck. We don't have to do anything but be; come into my space and just breathe.

I've never wanted someone so selfishly or been willing to love so selflessly. There is no room for me anymore. All I think about, all I see, you're all I want and all I need.

Come walk that walk and speak that beautiful talk. Sweet substances pour forth from your lips, a love language if I ever heard one. And even if I don't understand anything being said, I know *"I love you."*

Desire

I compose my thoughts of you into symphonies of escaped sounds
Soft cries of *yes* and *oh God* stay in my head
But they're all directed at you

My deep sighs and bruised lips are mere expressions of my feelings
So deep
So gentle the pursuit
But I am overcome by desire for you

These feelings are new and ready to be explored
Come here, let's get a room so I can learn your anatomy more…
You like to tease me and turn me on…
I just wanna return the favor

Kiss my lips and I'll bite yours
Hold my hips till they get sore
You've done something to me
I think I'm broken because all I see are replays of you.

You holding my hands
My waist
My face

You kissing my lips
My teeth
And the top of my tongue

You've got me frustrated in the worst way
Because only you can relieve me
Alleviate the aching and extinguish the fires that burn furiously
For you

It's all about you

My thoughts
Hopes
Desires
Fragrance

Shit… you've got me sprung

I've been caught in all my feels
Feels you've awakened
And guess what
I don't care

Kiss me, tease me, just promise to please me
I need it, I want it
I want you
Come soon to my side
I get a feeling you could make me come in tri's
Let's find out as we create sweet music
Our bodies the instruments
My body only plays music for you
All you gotta do is touch me and I'll hit a high C.
Come see

Te quiero.

Dearly Beloved

I can't think of anything else I'd rather do or anywhere else I'd rather be than with you. You, who makes me see things a bit more clearly. The fog of my heart sounds like a horn when you kiss me dearly.

Dearly beloved, I want to gather you up in my arms for always and eternity, and forever be capsized by your love when I let you in.
I hold onto the idea of forever, but this is a foreign concept that I haven't quite gripped yet as firmly as you have my waist.

It's for you that all these years I have remained chaste. I've watched and waited and waited and watched. I've never been able to really tell time on an analog clock, because the hand placement confused me.

And now I can feel the tick tick tick in my hip hip hip as your hands grip my side, caress my face, graze my thigh…kiss my lips, but don't pull back now because I love the way you taste.

You refresh me with words of affirmation and stroke my ego with gentle soliloquies that leave me counting my blessings.

Shit!

You make me hum. I hum the things my heart longs to speak,
but I can't bring proper utterance to. You got me thinking like the Song of Solomon and singing like Jill.

One day I'll help you feel as deeply as I do, but until then I'll wait.
Waiting for the hours on the clock to pass by slowly and assured,
Like the hands from your body as they caress mine. Or maybe I just imagined that. I can't tell the difference anymore.

Pay me no mind or give me it all. At this point I think I'll give you my all, so please be sure to catch me when I fall. You're the one I didn't know I was praying for. I have fallen for you and I can't get up; I don't want to.

Believe me when I say *I love you*. I pray that's enough.

Tease

When the man you love walks on by
Looking innocent
But is really anything but
And there is nothing you can do about it
But be flustered
And plan the time that you two make it right
Over and over again

Rock Around the Clock

Tick, tick, tick goes the body clock
Like my hips as they jeer you into submission.
You've got me wound tighter than a spring on the board of life
And I'm about to dive in
The time is almost right
And my body is feeling ripe.

My body clock is set with hands on 10 and 2,
Mind if I move them lower for you?
As the second-hand slips and lands gently on your…
Ensuring that you're ready for the hour at hand.

Tick!
Left hand at 10 and the other at 5,
At my waist you have arrived.
Left hand 7 and the other still at 5,
Sway with me as we dance to heaven.

Our hands circling one another slowly
Time going through every dimension and in every direction
Always going, never stopping
No two positions are ever the same no matter how many times we go around the clock.

Your hand grazes around back to wind me up,
Set my course off track.
Left hand is now at 12 and the other slowly tick, tick, ticks to 6,
And now my clock is broken because time has sped up to catch my breath.

In our recklessness,
You leave me breathless.
I must confess this,
I wish I could always have sex for breakfast.

You kiss 2 and I tick, tick, tick,
And twitch, twitch, twitch from the desire emanating between my hip, hip, hips.

I think you've broken me.
Your hands send me spiraling as they rock around the clock,
And I'm overheating with no end in sight.
Take your hand off my thigh,
I'm getting a little too high,
And I just need to think right.

Right hand on 2 and the other around back,
You wind me up to get me back on track.
This clock works just for you.
Keep winding me up and I'll never stop,
Rocking together until even time grows weary of our love.

To You

Hmmm, the things you make me feel when I'm around you I cannot explain. It's like my heart leaps out of my chest and attaches itself to yours. You make me feel like a clear summer day.

I drink your words like water, you bring me balance. When you smile at me…Lord! It's so beautiful and I get lost in it. When you look at me, it's like you're reading your favorite book. Taking your time so you don't miss anything.

The sound of your voice carries on the wind like the final note of a jazz song. Never hitting the ground, to be cherished because it is just that beautiful. Each word and declaration over my life to be savored because they are just that sweet.

And then we have your mind. Encased in brilliance. I promise you can teach me all night long. I'm a willing student. The way you break down complex topics into manageable structures is amazing. You're not just intelligent, but you are also wise. The wisdom you have puts me in the mind of Solomon. It makes me desire to let you lead me.

You are kind and that kindness washes away any cold front I may have been trying to put up. Of all the things you make me feel when I'm around you, I must honestly say, I feel loved and safe. Because of those two things I can't wait to walk with you forever.

Thirsty

I was thirsty,
Satan opened the tap.
In the search for water,
I ended up parched.

Genuine

Every day I prayed for *The One* who would find me.
I prayed that he would find me in purpose,
I didn't care whether it was by accident or on purpose.
I just never thought purpose looked like homelessness.
I always said I wanted to be so hidden in God that it would take God's help to find me,
And baby, that's exactly what happened.
You found me at my lowest,
Loved me at my worst,
You're learning my best,
And I want you to know you're all I want and need above the rest.

In those jeans is a phone I'd like to toss from time to time.
Especially when it's in the bed.
In those jeans, there's the sexiest ass I've had the pleasure of making an acquaintance with.
There are back dimples that smile when I poke them.
Between those legs that are strong enough to run up Van Ness from Market Street,
There is your *"friend"* who is more than capable and willing to rock me to sleep.

In those jeans walks a man of integrity and strength.
There is authority and headship in the man within those jeans.
You walk confidently with a swagger that makes my *"friend"* tremble and my knees go weak.
Those jeans cover the shoes that clothe strong feet that bear the weight they carry.
You carry yourself well my love.
You carry your burdens with grace and diligence and I love you.
I love you for fighting.
I love you for loving me.

In those genes, there are the brownest eyes that see into my soul
and make me melt with a glance.
There is something about you that drives me to candor.
There is a smile connected to the eyes that caress my face,
And there are lips that I love to taste
Right next to the dimple that smiles back at me as you expose your beautiful teeth.

In those genes, there is the most beautiful mix of melanin I've ever had the pleasure of kissing.
The hues of caramel and mocha that line your left arm
Are like the oceans that do not cross,
But stand magnificent and majestic in their meeting.
I'd like to trace that meeting place with my tongue. *(One day soon)*

My fingers get lost in that beautiful head of hair
Causing me to lose my head
As you rest yours on my chest and bury your face into my neck.
I swear I was made just for you and you for me.

One day when those jeans come off,
Our genes will meet
And create the most beautiful thing we've ever seen;
The best of you and the best of me.

I could go on forever about my love and admiration for you,
But I will close in saying this:
Thank you for being diligent and allowing God to form your character
For such a time as this.
There isn't one day that I regret coming to SF.
You make it worth it more and more
Every day I get to be with you.
Thank you.
I love you.

What Do You See?

When you look at me, what do you see?

Who do you see,
The real me or just my outer beauty?

I'm more than a pretty face and tiny waist.
If you want me, you must want *all* of me.

Can you handle that?
Handle me?
Hold me?

When I feel broken and come undone,

Will you still be there?

You Don't See Me

You look right at me, but you don't see me. You don't understand the significance of who we are to one another. Or who we are supposed to be anyway. Maybe it's youthful immaturity. Perhaps your fears and nerves cloud your good judgement. It could be that you just don't care. You say you're my friend, my "brother," but family doesn't treat one another like this. Constantly missing cues and opportunities to make amends. I often feel rejected by you. Cast away and not thought of until you need me, or something of me. Yet I still see the good in you although you don't see me at all.

Shoot Straight

Ugh!

                                      All I want is transparency.

Let your yes be yes,

                                          Your no be no.
                                   I'm so sick of maybe,

Tired of sorry.

                                     Soon is an eternity
                            That never seems to come.

Stop dragging me

                                                   A
                                    R
                O
                U
                            N
                                               D

                    Just shoot straight.

Disarmed

It's alarming how quickly you disarm me. I sharpen my weapons to cut you down to size and then you stroll in coolly and strip me of every quip and biting word I may have thought of before. The edge is immediately lost from my words as your lips against melt mine.

Dammit!

I hate that I can't stay mad, can't stay sad. You make me glad, giving me the love and attention I've always wanted, but never had.

It's so alarming how quickly you disarm me. Your eyes speak volumes to my soul and when you tell me to come I listen. I can't fight you. Believe me, I've tried. Our disagreements dissolve too quickly to give me too long of a pause.

I know you.

I've known bullshit, and you don't fit the description. You keep me on my toes and have my ears and eyes opened.
I see you and I love you. It scares me that I do, so tread softly.
My heart is fragile as it lies in your hands, I trust you *almost* completely.

Keep your eyes on me and they'll tell you some truths. They're salted with "be patient with me" and "I love you." Hold on and don't let go, even when I pull away. It just means I need you to pull me back and try again.

You make me feel things I'm not well aquatinted with and that scares me. You infuriate me in the best ways and defuse my thoughts with expert precision. You must belong here because no one has scaled my wall so quickly and effortlessly.

I love you, and it scares me, so I fight myself more than I fight you.

Be patient, mi amor. It took me a while to get here, and now that you're here I'm not going anywhere.

Mírame

I love that look. It tells me you love me, silently. Wordlessly and breathlessly, we exchange confirmations of love. I hold your neck, and you my waist. I kiss your lips to get a taste.

I pull back slowly because this atmosphere we've created is like a well-formed bubble unbreakable in its fragility. The space between us isn't fully realized because you may leave me physically, but it doesn't add up to a hill of beans compared to the mountains I've climbed for you.

Keep looking at me like you love me, and I'll tell you. Show me you love me, and I'll show you.

Show Me

I get put through shit to grow closer to you. Our conversation in BK was much needed and successful in comparison to our other talks. I feel like you're actually listening and getting it.

I hold out on my kisses, and you tell me you need them. I hear what I need to hear, an apology, and I give up my defenses. You tease me with your kisses and drive me up a wall and I love and dislike you for it. You infuriate me in ways only you can. I'm so glad I ran into you on the street. It wasn't by chance. I walked two blocks thinking "why didn't I catch a bus?" and then I saw you and I knew it was perfect timing because I ran into you. What a pleasant surprise.

Your sound when you spoke as we parted touched my ears and reached into my core. And that look though… It said, "I love you. Don't leave me. I need you." It melted me long before you even took me into your arms. I took note and now hold onto the memory of that look, the sound of you, and the feeling it gave me. A feeling of closure and longing.

You make me love you simply by being you. I look at you and I fall in love all over again. Over and over again I find myself falling. My spirit leaps when I see you, recognizing my other half while longing to be reunited.

Getting It Right

All this time I had it all wrong.
See, I was praying and begging for God to change you,
To get you to notice me.
When instead I need you to notice Him,
And I need Him to change me.
I was so busy holding grudges because I couldn't hold your hand.
Too conceited and proud to realize that I needed God to deal with me before I could be ready for you.
I love you, don't doubt that ever
But I was trying to love you the best I knew how.
Now I'm letting God show me how to love you, so I'll be exactly what you need.
All this time I had it wrong.
But now I'm getting it right.

I Stepped Back

I stepped back, and you stepped up.
You opened yourself to God allowing Him to work in you.
Now soon we can step in sync.

The Shift

There has been a shift, I can see it.
You speak differently, tread differently…
You look different, yet still recognizable and oh so desirable.

You no longer seem like a boy, a boy continually mangling my heart with silence and inaction.
Today I saw that perhaps you are a man like you constantly proclaim.

The best part, you came to me as a friend.
We had a conversation; I've missed those.
You showed me I am worth your time.
Maybe… there is hope for us yet.

This Is New

Maybe it's true that absence makes the heart grow fonder
I don't know but I do know that I miss you when you're not around.

Maybe love at first sight is real
This I know is true because every time I see you it's like I'm seeing you for the first time, and I keep falling in love with you each time.

When I saw you the last time I felt like I knew you yet did not know you.
Something about you changed, in a good way.
You gave me butterflies, I'm not used to those.

When you touched me, it felt familiar yet brand new.
You ministered to me when I didn't even know I was empty and needed you.

You are the glue that holds me down.
I guess what I'm trying to say is,
This is new...

A Rib Out of Place

My spirit lights up when I'm around you.
When we're apart, it cries tears so deep and complex
My mind and eyes can't fathom them.
Tears near the surface but never coming out.
Because my natural man cannot begin to understand
What it feels like to be a rib out of place.
I want to be beside you but instead we are further apart than before.
I'm waiting until I can be where I belong.
Which is wherever you are.
I miss you.
I need you.
I love you.

30 Minutes

30 Minutes. That's all it took to disarm me completely, to erase the hurts, the pains, the worry, the doubts, the fears.

Everything about us was comfortable with one another as we slipped back into our old routine. Me picking things out of your beard and hair and you presenting your latest theory. As we sat there I kept scanning you to take a mental picture, something for my mind to remember until the next time I see you. When we hugged I breathed in your familiar scent and I smiled, grateful it hadn't changed.

I bet that you also knew there was more than one conversation taking place at that table. While I heard you in the natural, the conversation in the spirit was much more intriguing. It was as though two halves of a whole were reassembling themselves while also bracing for the separation that was sure to come.

It was only 30 minutes but what was lacking was restored. I was strengthened by you while also lending you strength I didn't know I had. What have you done to me? What have I done to you? What are we doing to one another? Whatever it is, promise me it will never stop.

30 minutes seemed like a lifetime. I'm looking forward to the many lifetimes I get to spend with you.

The Sound of My Thoughts

As I embark on this new season I feel out of pocket. Nothing seems right. The feeling I have is numbness, reminiscent of Novocain. I am lost without you but maybe I'm just as lost with you. It's been two nights and two days without so much as an, "are you okay?" I know I'm not the only one feeling lost, left out, left behind. All you must do is reach out to me, I'm here waiting to be found. I'm not going anywhere. Until then, I fall asleep to the sound of my thoughts of you, until I have the pleasure of hearing your voice again.

Longing

My longing for you has changed.
I desire you on a level that I haven't ever wanted anyone else.
I want and need you next to me.
If all we did was lay together and watch the Sunset,
That would be alright with me
I miss you and long to see you again;
It's been much too long.

Sunrise

I lay here after a night of tossing and turning watching the sunrise knowing that right about now you're on your way to work. We're both watching the same sunrise from two different vantage points and perspectives but still it's the same sky.

Though the beauty of the sunrise has nothing on you. On the way your eyes light up when you're happy, or how you show emotion with your whole body. You light up my life like the sun the sky but when you're not around my life seems overcast and gray. Things that I find beautiful look a little less spectacular when you're not around.

I'm looking forward to when the sun rises in my life again. It's not the same without you.

What I Miss Most

My new place is great.
It has peace, quiet, a magnificent view of the city.
The only thing that it's missing is you.
Your smile, your laugh, your jokes, your fragrance.
Your very presence.

I miss the way my spirit lights up as well as my eyes every time you come around.
I miss your animated gestures.
I miss the scans of one another we often do yet try and pretend we don't.
I miss your hugs, the lingering ones where you bury your head in my shoulder.
I miss the feel of you in my arms pressed against me.
I miss constantly tidying you up.
I miss everything about you.

I don't know if this will ever feel like home
Without you here with me.

Sacrifices

Countless times I've waited,
Hoping,
Anticipating your every move,
Your wants, hopes, and desires,
And I get shit.

Sacrifice upon sacrifice.

I sit and give, and give, and give,
My time, my money, my mind, my body.

Don't waste my time.
My body is now a battle ground.
My mind seems to be playing tricks on my body
Telling me I don't need you.
That I don't want you.
Not your mind, your smile, or body.
Not your courage, your integrity, your heart.
Nope.

I don't trust your judgement,
Don't trust your word.
I've become a "show me" woman
Because I just don't know anymore.

Give me distance.
Give me what's due to me.
Get right dammit!
I'm tired of waiting
Of sacrificing
Of suffering
Of feeling like we're missing out on the best that we could be.

You make me feel undervalued and like my time isn't appreciated.

And yet I love you.
It hurts.
It hurts to love you because love hurts.
It's not easy to love and be loved
And you teach me that every day.

How sweet it would be to be perfectly loved by you.
Until then, yet again, I wait.
Patiently impatient.
Impregnated?
Happy belated…
You should feel congratulated.

Five W's

I spent a whole day:
Watching people push past poverty,
Wishing for fleeting florescent flashes of reciprocated feeling,
Wanting the influx of impish and inconsiderate impulses to decrease.
I waited.
Wasted a whole day.

The Beginning of the End

He sits there looking on smugly as I stare down at my nails. They're too long. Well, not actually but they're not the shape I need them to be. They're that weird squoval shape that I file so hard to get rid of. That in between square and oval. Like the damn things couldn't make up their minds about what they wanted to be. I need definitive. I'd be ok with a short, rounded nail, or a long, square, "I'll – cut – you – if – I – want – to" nail. They're just not right.

Kinda like the felling I have in my gut right now. The one that tells me I'm in deep shit. The one that usually leaves me questioning, "How the hell did I get here?" and "How do I get out with some dignity?" Fuck dignity, just get me outta here. I don't even remember what he asked me, but I know he didn't like my response.

"It's not your decision."

I can tell by the tone I hear. The words are unimportant. That tone says, "Fuck your tears." Wait. He just told me not to cry. I guess I read the tone correctly. So now I sit here and stifle my sniffles because I refuse to let anything else show.

Why am I here right now? Why is he still here? Sitting so smug. Like a little shit – "_____."

He's calling my name. I used to like the way it sounded on his lips, though I am accustomed to the ever-affectionate term "bae." Now it's "_____." No longer warm and familiar. My name coming from him is now like butter sizzling over grated coals. Somewhere along the way we've gotten up. We're walking now. I can only tell because of the fresh air reviving me and the change of scenery. He leaves for work and I walk away, numb and struck dumb.

Unsteady

My thoughts are a little unsteady right now going between anger and hurt caused by you and the love I feel towards you. I wonder if you worry about me a fraction as much as I worry about you. Even if it was just a tiny percentage, it would still be a lot because you consume 100% of my thoughts.

I haven't heard a word from you. So, I have no way of knowing if you feel as poorly as I do. If you're sorry. If you even care. I feel a bit unsteady because I feel like I'm on a rollercoaster with you. Which I find terrifying and I know you do too.

Just when I think that things are on the up, you drop me.
I feel like I'm drowning, choking on tears I didn't know I had left to cry. I don't cry often but lately it's been often because of you.
Feeling adrift riding a wave of complex emotions with no chance of stability in sight. I keep lending you a hand to only have it brushed away. You know you have my heart, yet you don't take care to look after it.

I'm feeling unsteady. I just want my thoughts and emotions to stop spinning. I'm tired of going around in circles. When will this dance end?

Rest

My eyes burn
from the countless hours they spent
staring into the artificial light on my phone.

Too many conversations held via text.
Not enough face to face communication.

Not enough *love*...
      if there was any at all.

Now that I have walked away,
you want to be attentive.
Nah...miss me with that.

It's your turn to lay awake at night
and struggle with
"to sleep, or not to sleep."

To receive a text, is to *breathe*...
      but now is your turn to suffocate,

because I've decided
      to come up for air.

The air is free up here, and that is how I plan to stay.
Keep your ill-timed emotions to yourself.
They're not valued here.

It's time for me to turn over the phone,
turn over in my bed,
and *rest*.

Knowing that, as twisted as it was
      I passed this test.
The best, is yet to come.

Broken(ness)

They never mention the heartbreak you feel when you breakup with someone.
The pain of being the one to say *"I can't do this anymore."*
I loved you once,
Still do,
And yet,
I know I will hate you if I don't leave you.
I cried so many times on your behalf.
And I thought I was done,
But it seems the well is plentiful.

I forgave you this morning,
Truly forgave you
And even with my grievances aired and hurts released,
There was still some pain left behind waiting to be expelled.

I'm broken.

I've heard that God can use broken things,
Mend them to their original intent and make them beautiful.
Now I guess it's my turn.
My brokenness is showing.
Please…
Make me beautiful.

Hearts Don't Break

They crack
And splinter
Hearts are wounded
But they don't break
Instead they are mended haphazardly by the owner
As they hope it still works.

Love Hurts

I was told to love you, which I did I guess but I guess I missed the how.
I thought it was eros but maybe it was just supposed to be philia.
You don't understand that behind my smile are tears I refuse to cry.
I don't want to allow you to join the ranks of men that hurt me because I still want to be able to care about you.
You see, in my loving you it's hurting me.
I think you're worth everything, even risking my embarrassment to show you that.
Yet it seems that to you, I'm not even worth the truth.

Love hurts, but is it supposed to?
Why do we insist on doing things that are wounding us?

Twice the Fool

They ask, "why do fools fall in love?"
I, for all the wisdom I thought I had, seem to have played the fool…twice.
Two times I let people get too close.
I only had one rule, protect my heart and never let anyone close enough to wound it.
I betrayed myself by letting my guard down and my feelings out.
How reckless could I be?
Perhaps I moved too fast?
Or more likely I am just destined to do life solo;
That's fine I guess.
You know,
I allowed myself to fall because I liked the idea of love
And that someone could feel that way towards me.
But I guess the only one who can feel that towards me,
Is me.

Letting Go

Wow…

I let you go, and you've danced back into my life.
Flittered back into my heart and set my emotions aflutter

I'm a flusterfuck of emotion
and it's all because of you.

I've waited so long for you
So long to tell you I love you
So long to sing to you
To hold you up when you can't stand on your own

It's been so long since I've said, so long.

Hello again
I've missed your face
Your smile and the way it lights up your eyes.

You're too kind my love
Do you mind if I call you that?

Because it's certainly true.
I do miss and love you.
I can't wait to fall *in love* with you.
It's a daunting feat but I'm willing to take the leap
Because I've waited for you.
Fought for you.
Suffered for you.
Loved and lost for you.

It's time.

Old Friend

I am the crease in your forehead that gives you pause.

You've been more affectionate to me lately.
This is usually a solitary place where I get a hand or two for a checkup, or two fingers for pimple popping, but today I've been given special treatment.

Today I've been caressed by all five fingers and graced with the back of the palm.
You must really love me today.
It must be my birthday!

I forgive you for neglecting me all these weeks.
I can't see the rest of the face as we are all separate, but as I look at the face across from mine, I see a mouth set in a frown line.
That can't be good…

That line is usually the other way around, and come to think of it, you neglect me when that line is right side up…
That face must be the cause of my unexpected affection and neglect.
I'm grateful for that face right now.

It got me my old friend back.

Good News

Life drags in good things with the bad, and bad with the good.

I came across an opportunity the other day, and the only person I could think of sharing it with, was you. You, who hadn't made it clear that you never intended to be here for me.

I waited, paced, and pondered. I cursed, and shook my first, and wondered and wandered around town with this good news on the tip of my tongue. But, I couldn't release the words, as weighty as they were on my tongue.

So, I left a half-heartedly petty message. Passive aggressive in my disappointment, hopeful in my intentions.

But you…you had the ball in your court and decided to drop it. It's been seven weeks now. It's safe to say, I've moved on.

Friend Zone

I find myself in the

                              FRIENDZONE...

I hate it!
Especially because we both know
there is more than friendship between us.
Yet, we go on as though nothing has changed
But everything has changed.
Expectations are unclear
Feelings are muddled
I find myself pining after you
Since you stay on my mind.
I know I shouldn't because
You're just a... "friend."
Caught in the middle of mixed emotions I wonder,
Will I ever gain my status back?

How to Be Just Friends

You wanted a situationship and ended up in the Friend Zone. You wanted to be "just friends" but you seem to have forgotten the role you chose to play. Let me help you remember.

1. Stop trying to slide in my DMs.
2. The only benefit you'll be getting is my company…and even that is a maybe.
3. Don't text me after ten.
4. No mixed message emojis (**NO** 😳, 🍑, 🍆, or 🍒!)
5. Or conversations dripping with innuendo.
6. Realize that my heart is not to be toyed with.
7. Stay in your lane.

It's Complicated

We have become a generation where *"it's complicated"* has become an acceptable relationship status.
Why is that?
What exactly is so complicated?
It's either you are, or you aren't.
They're either yours or you're trifling.
Let's replace complicated with committed.
If they won't commit it's time to dip.
Watch how quickly that'll simplify your life.

For Free? *(Nigga Please!)*[1]

This pussy ain't free!

It's valued at more than dinner and dancing.
Although, the right meal and song choice might make the price more appealing.
Who told you I would give it up for a free meal
And some mediocre conversation from a *would be, should be,* gentleman?
Didn't you know?
Weren't you informed?
That's just the down payment,
Not the entrance fee.

This pussy ain't free!

It's worth more than the ten-dollar trimmer that it took to tame it.
It's worth far more than the piece of rump roast steak I've become in your eyes.
It's when it's loaned out for daily specials,
That the wholesale price gets misconstrued.
Just because one decided to sell for the low, low, doesn't mean everyone is the same price.
And don't mistake the price and the value you've assigned to her.

You're not paying for your satisfaction.
You're not paying to get in and get off.
You're paying her dowry,
And the value of self-esteem
And every inch of pure magic attached to the woman.
You're paying for the sound of her voice in adoration.
You're paying for the sound of laughter being shared with you

---

[1] Inspired by Kendrick Lamar's "For Free."

Instead of being cast on your lapel at your expense.

But wait...I almost forgot my audience

Y'all like that free, no questions asked, "pass the peas" pussy.
Get in where you fit in and maybe your friend can too pussy.
But this,
This shit right here...this ain't free my nigga.

I paid the price to get where I am, to be who I am.
So who the hell do you think you are to get my most valued gift for free?
Ha!
I laugh on your lapel.

Best believe, if you want me you're gonna have to pay the price.
Shit, I had to pay and it belongs to me.
But guess what?
That's the way it is, and will always be because,

This pussy ain't free!

Situationship

I like many have found myself in a situationship at one time or another.
A situationship where the situation was that we were both too co-dependent to relinquish our attachment to one another.
We instead toyed with each other's emotions
Playing each other like a fiddle
Demanding things we didn't have the right to expect
Yet not willing to define ourselves.

We sent mixed signals
Coded so well that no one could decipher them,
Including us.
We continued in this vein for two years
Not wanting to hold on but afraid to let go.
Wanting more but terribly afraid of change.

Then, circumstance ended the situationship.
Yet I still found myself studying and re-reading your texts as though they were sacred,
Feeling as though I could never say goodbye,
Silently wondering if this was the end, knowing that it was.
Looking back, I'm grateful for the end of our situationship.

We both deserve so much more.

I Gave You Agape

Hoping to get eros and got ludus in return. It was all fun and games to you, even when I got hurt. In trying to love you, I neglected philautia. Self-care was secondary, you were my primary focus. Yet I was your option. The one you turned to on a rainy day. Looks like you're about to experience a drought. I gave you agape, hoping to get eros. I was misguided, trading one, hoping to get the other, receiving neither. Now, we can't even have philia, our friendship ruined by the lies you told. I hope whomever you choose next, they don't get the same empty, "I love you," that you gave me.

X Factor

You tried to keep our relationship X over zero
treating it as though it was *i*.

You refused to factor me in,
never raised me to a higher degree,
no exponential growth.

So, I substituted you out
for someone who was willing to go through the process to solve
for me.

No shortcuts needed.

I thought you were my conjugate
but every problem with you ended irrationally.
You were in your prime, allowing no one in
but yourself.

So, I subtracted you and added him
leaving you wondering why you're the ex- factor.

Possibilities

The atmosphere is changing
I can see the lines drawn
A definitive before and after of this tipping point
Yet I am not off balance
Actually, I'm quite steady
So much unknown around me
Yet I'm not fighting it
I see the choice between control, comfort
And freedom to explore
To grow
To know
Do I settle
If I do will I settle well
Or do I try something way beyond my imagination and scope
I owe it to myself
I've asked for it and well,
Here it is
Do I take it or…
Leave it as a pleasant possibility

As It Was in the Beginning

I was Ruth when you first saw me
Invested in purpose
So caught up in my own plans
I didn't recognize you.

When I noticed your desire for me,
I became the Shulamite woman
Worried about my appearance to you
Lacking much, so I thought
Yet you called me a rose among thorns.

You called me out of hiding.
Guiding me and teaching me
As it was in the beginning.

The Waiting

The waiting was the hardest part.
I looked for you, knowing that I wasn't supposed to but,
I was too restless to be at rest.
I knew that you were supposed to find me
But that it's hard to locate a moving target.

I played double-dutch with my heartstrings
While my thoughts and emotions were on a never ending merry go round of
Is he or isn't he…
Will he or won't he…

Every time someone who wasn't you looked my way
I rushed to the throne to ask, *"is he The One?"*
I almost settled for the counterfeits,
Not one but three
Because I had settled within myself that you weren't coming.

Until you showed up one day
Helping me detangle myself from useless attachments fueled by my insecurities
Now it feels like heaven, something from a dream
But the waiting was the hardest part.

> *With the close of our relationship,*
> *You made counterfeit number four.*
> *You detangled me to ensnare me again.*
> *I'm done looking for "The One."*
> *Instead, I'm finally content in singleness.*
> *Waiting is the hardest part, true.*
> *I don't mind it anymore.*

Until Next Time

I sit hastily wiping away tears as my mind replays thoughts of you. I'm not sure what's going on with me, I wish I did. I know it has something to do with you and the change you represent. I work to gather my emotions and streamline my thoughts. We'll see each other again, in time. Until then, I hope you think of me as I of you. Smiling as we reflect on things only we know.

I Know

I know that I have a lot to learn
But I know you'll teach me.
As much as I have to learn
I have that much to offer.

I know that you are straight forward
I'll always get honesty from you.
I'll give you the same,
Even when it hurts.

I know that you love me
But I don't know if you know
I love you too
Because it's hard for me to open up and show it.

I know that you're *The One*
The promise
Not a reincarnation of every man that's hurt me.
You are what I have prayed for.

I know that you know,
This is all new for me.
Forgive me if I move slowly
But thank you for your patience.

Redeemed

Forgive me if I seem…standoffish…or unsure of what I want. I know what I want, I want you. But, I have reservations. See, I need you to understand, there were three before you I who thought were you. They said they were you, but they were counterfeits, Ishmaels, learning tools, to prepare me for you.

One wanted to ravish my spirit, another my money, the last, my body. They each left with a part of me that didn't belong to them. I've recovered these things, but it took some time.

You, you're different…I hope. You watched me, waiting to say hello. I can see you helping to restore those broken places. We'll create new memories to erase the past. What is the past when we have now? You saw me and took your shot. Making clear your aim.

Redemption.

Once again
Attracted to fool's gold.
Thankfully,
There is redemption in the Lord
Because these men
Were of the fallen angel variety.

Fear

I'm spiraling and it's making me dizzy
Going back and forth, playing parkour with my thoughts
Allowing my emotions to bounce around like pinball
Emotionally backed up because I've closed off, too afraid to be vulnerable
Worrying if I am doing too much, or if maybe I'm not doing enough
I just wish that I could tell you
Tell you how I feel
How much you mean to me
How much I want to be with you
That I miss you
That I love you
I could, all it would take is a text or a phone call, but I don't
I never say it
Too afraid that silence will be my answer
I'm sorry I've allowed fear and doubt to join our relationship
Both trying to get me to self-sabotage and walk away
Hold me please, until I become okay

Love TKO

I'm in the ring of love
My challenger isn't the object of my desire
He sits watching from the sidelines
Seeing if I truly think he's worth fighting for
My opposition isn't Satan
No, my opponent is me
It's my spirit versus my flesh
One wishes to wrap itself in what once was
The other looking eagerly towards what could be
I tire myself out fighting myself
Wounding myself by continually rehashing prior hurts
Just knowing they will happen again
Except they won't
Unless I speak them into being
He's not every other guy
And he's worth fighting for
So, I'm going to knock down my flesh
And make it take several seats
A TKO before my fears TKO me

My flesh needed to have several seats,
But not for the reasons I thought.
Both spirit and flesh were knocked out.
Deception was in the ring
And I didn't even know it.

I Will Pray for You

I will pray for you
Calling on the name of someone you don't believe in…yet.

I will not pray that you are *"The One."*
Instead, I'll pray that you be who God needs you to be to me
You think religion and faith make you weak.
Well, then I am weak in the knees because of you
Because on them I will stay
Because you're worth it.
There is a level of love more intimate than sex;
It's prayer.

You've asked to share my body,
I'm going to share with you a greater gift,
What I've been holding close and reluctant to share.
The body is but a vessel,
Holding the spirit.
Mine will keep steady intercession for yours.
It's sleeping,
But not for much longer.

Until you wake,
I will pray for you.

> *I prayed for you and the signs manifested,*
> *Red flags all around.*
> *You were not The One, not even close.*
> *A wolf in sheep's clothing wanting to ravish me.*
> *How did you hide your fangs?*
> *I almost let you, because I was willing to settle.*
> *I was afraid of the truth,*
> *Using you as a deflection,*
> *To help keep myself*
> *In self-deception.*

Trauma

Trauma sneaks upon the unexpecting like a thief in the night. It calmly crashes in, leaving the body paralyzed and the mind in turmoil. Sometimes it's so subtle, it's not detected. You've conformed to it, wrapping it around yourself like a security blanket.

You show bravado, you act bold, but daily your only goal is to outrun a past that isn't even chasing you because trauma has chained you to it. Nightmares, night scares, aggression, anxiety all because every time you close your eyes you see the lies trauma tries to create.

It tries to overwhelm you and drag you backwards. You start to dull with it, almost entirely submerged until you realize, you have the power to break the chain.

Settling

People think they will settle well,
They won't.

We settle as well as oil and water…
Is it worth it, to settle, because the weight is too great?

Just wait.

Choices

I can get with this new thing that God is doing, or I can futility chase after that which God has ended.
But I'm afraid to choose the new
Because of what that option makes me feel.
Because it makes me feel at all.
Choices.
What am I going to do?
My mind says no, slow down, this isn't real.
But my heart says yes, and it wants what it wants.

Denial

I claim to be woke but allow areas of my life to remain comatose.
Ready and willing to push everyone away
for fear that *The Right One*
may look like…
Me.

A Heart Under Construction

I have put a keep out sign on my heart.
It is closed until further notice.
I've constantly opened my heart to the wrong people.
All they've done is take, I've got to guard the fragments I have left.

It's wise to guard your heart but then how can construction begin?
How can restoration happen if you won't let Elohim in?
Refusing to let go of the building materials, the fragments you hold dear,
Slows down the process and doesn't allow you to be healed.

But you just don't understand the depth of the pain I feel!
The levels of hurt that Elohim would have to wade through to make me whole again.
It's too much to deal with, too painful to bear.
I… I just can't go there.

Can't or won't?
You can run but you cannot hide.
Elohim can heal you if you allow,
But you must first let go of what keeps you bound.

Decidedly Whole

My emotions were scattered, my heart unhinged.
Time passed by the wounds you left,
but didn't heal it.

My mind lay in fragments
while my soul drifted into depression un-noticed.
I wondered how I got so caught up in your potential,
that I was potentially willing to settle for you.
I neglected to guard the thing you inevitably broke,
but didn't know you had
Because it was a situationship.

I got tired of breaking up with men I wasn't dating.
Those who selfishly kept me waiting without a word,
their only imprint my newest wound.
Leaving me to break the ties around my soul,
that carried me to places I thought I had left behind.

To get free was a decision
To keep my heart open to Gods will, terrifying.

It took time;
it took God.

He loved me unconditionally,
Held me while I cried,
Assured me that His best is out there,
Waited for me to trust Him again, fully,
Encouraging me to believe in love again,
To believe that I could be loved.

That made all the difference.

Love You

Love you,
No I attached.
Words used as a cover
Sounding close enough to the real thing.
Words used to convey an emotion
I'm not sure I understand.

Love you,
No I attached.
Removing myself
To protect against a hurt
That never came.

While I was protecting myself,
I was missing out,
Too afraid to add the I,
To emotionally invest myself and be all in.
Instead, just, love you.

But how could I love you
If I didn't love me?
How could you love me,
When you didn't know all of me?
I know you didn't
Because not even I truly knew myself.

I wonder,
What I've been missing
By giving the illusion of being all in
While still withholding
Almost all of myself.

I Used to Love to Hate Her

I used to love to hate her... the young woman staring back at me in the mirror.
The person I hated to look at but had to face, daily.

My shadow, my first enemy, my reluctant friend.

I stared at her, fault finding.
Beating her down until I saw a subdued masked version of her.
Under the mask were bruises inflicted by my own hand.
My tongue cutting her deeper than the words of others ever could.

Spirit broken, soul gashed.

All because she knew me...the *real* me,
The less than perfect walking contradiction,
The hypersensitive hypocrite with abandonment issues.

Hiding but wanting to be seen, *needing* to be seen.

I took the stones thrown at me and built a fortress,
Locking her inside away from the public eye.

I divorced myself from myself.

I insisted on walking around disjointed
Afraid to face those imperfections that spoke of a process that led me to maturity.
Instead, playing tug of war with the lies I told myself
To justify the mistreatment of what took God care to create.
Trying so hard to cut ties with those who had eyes to see through me.
Who wanted to help detangle me because my fortress had become a prison,
The ropes a noose.

I didn't want to hear it
Convinced that I am all wrong while badly pretending to be alright.

I tried to push her away from me,
Tiring myself out while digging in my heels.
It was like trying to get a mountain to move
Or the sky to change position.

I felt that freedom was too expensive
Because it would require me to cash out my shame, my pain, the things I so closely held on to.

I used to love to hate her.
Until I realized,
Hating her was killing me…

I'm not ready to die yet.

Fortress

I built a fortress with every stone thrown at me. Encasing myself in a scripted narrative. That I had to walk the church's prescribed path to see God. Many will be surprised when they miss Heaven for raising Hell. Stone by stone, the fortress will come down. I'm coming out, no going back, no more tug of war. You don't have to accept me, but I do.

Reclaiming

I'm taking back everything.
My body, my spirit, my peace of mind.
I'm taking back my joy, and I'm going to blossom when you thought I would wilt without you.
You don't control my season.
I'm reclaiming the essence of myself,
Strength, wit, and sass.
I refuse to carry the baggage you left behind.
I've discarded it.
I'm tired of being a bag lady.
Reclaiming my time, reclaiming my heart,
Focused on just doing me.

Healing

Tonight,
I look a look at myself and liked what I saw.
I treated myself nicely.
Cleansing myself from head to toe,
Layers of debris coming off me.
Down the drain went the fingerprints of every man that has hurt me.
I erased the words of those trying to make me into *their* image.
I smiled
As I ran my hands through the memories of obstacles overcome
Moving them to make space for the new.
Anointing myself,
Speaking life to areas of my body that lay dry, desolate
I began loving myself.
And that is when the healing came.

Freedom

I wish I had paid closer attention to the indifference you so carefully hid. The absence of hands touching and gazes that no longer held affection.

Questions were still asked with measured skepticism and weighed with feigned concern. I wish my eyes were open the whole time, not half closed with contentment, now wide open and cloaked in resentment.

But I forgive you.

Never mistake that choice having been made for you. I made it for *me*.

And now, *I am free*.

A Letter to My Ex

We could've been great.
We could've made it.
But 3 arguments,
6 tests,
And 1 decision later...
We are no more.
And I wouldn't change a thing.
I wanted all 6 results to be positive, so I could prove you wrong,
Prove God right,
Not sound crazy or hysterical.
Because who in their right mind takes the words of God over the results of scientific facts?
I did.
And you called me crazy.
Told me I should go back to church, so they could fix me with their controlling ways.
And that even if I was indeed pregnant,
I should *"deal with it."*

So...
I did.
I got rid of you lol.
Turns out I'm not nor have I ever been pregnant,
But during the time that I was led to believe otherwise I was torn between wanting it to belong to you and not wanting you to be a part of the process at all.
I was in emotional turmoil partially feeling like "fuck you" but "I love you".

That's where I was.
Almost a year later, I'm so much better now.
I still question why I was led to believe such a thing could happen to me,

And I may never get an answer.
But I still wouldn't change a thing.
I will always believe God over anything I see hear or feel,
Because if I didn't,
You, my fellow reader, wouldn't be reading these words today.

Love and Lost

Is it better to have loved and lost than to have never loved at all?

Both hurt the same.
Few know the pains of love until they have loved someone in vain

Is it better to have loved and lost than to have never loved at all?

Was it ever even love
Or was it lust, cleverly disguised, a cheap imitation?

I Forgive You

I spent my time on you. Knowing that there would be no refunds, I settled for brief exchanges.

My time was treated as meaningless as I was left waiting and wondering. My emotions grew weary and my heart cold.

You made me feel as though I wasn't enough, not spiritual enough, pretty enough, as though as I was less than. I've seen the girls you've chosen, or would choose, while denying me the opportunity of closure.

I used to say that you made me insecure but then I realized, *I don't have to eat everything that I'm served.*

For everything I was put through, I forgive you. The time spent, not wasted, showed me the type of woman I was, and the type of woman I don't want to be.

Scars

Scars can be a beautiful thing
It means that you've lived life
Instead of letting life have its way with you
What tried to kill you/didn't/ it made you stronger

There is no need to be ashamed of your scars
It shows you didn't stay wounded
But instead were able to heal
It takes strength to take life by the horns
And conquer instead of being its victim

We all have scars
Some are visible while others are buried deep within
It doesn't matter how you got them
They are a part of you now
An are an irreplaceable part of your story

All warriors carry battle scars
You may have gone through many wars
But you emerged victorious
Each scar is a testament that
The test didn't break you

Your scars don't define you
But they are part of you
They're in your past but helped shape your present
Scars can be a beautiful thing
Because they tell stories words never can.

To Those Who Hurt

Teardrops falling like rain, cascading down with no end in sight
Grief grips your soul rendering you unable to feel, not wanting to live
Yet live you must and so you do the minimum to keep the questions at bay
Day after day
Though the tears may never leave your eyes, they are always close to the surface
Many feel that it's their fate to live this way in pain
God never intended for us to live hurt
He comprehends and collects our tears as prayers, even when we're too tired to make a sound
Jesus understands our hurt, He's been hurt in every way.
He understands our tears because He himself has wept.
He was hurt so that we can be free from the pain.
Though life may bite and sting the love of God is the antidote
Stop drinking the poison of pain and be soothed by His touch.
To those who hurt, know it doesn't have to be a permanent state.
Grief and sorrow may endure for a night
But joy will come in the morning one you embrace the light.

About the Author – Sarai W.

Website: www.saraiwaters.com
Instagram: @tosaraiwithlove

Sarai W. - Sarai is a poet, singer, songwriter, and author. She was born and raised on the East Coast where she earned her B.A. in Theater from South Carolina State University. Sarai then moved to the West Coast to complete her M.A. in Film and Media from the New York Film Academy in Burbank, CA. Following the completion of her M.A., Sarai relocated to San Francisco, CA, immersing herself in the poetry scene there. Sarai presently resides in Atlanta, GA.

About the Author – Just Duléa

Website:
www.conviction2change.com/justdulea
Instagram/Twitter/Facebook:
@Justdulea

Just Duléa – Just Duléa is an author, songwriter, and spoken word artist from the East Coast. She is the Founder/CEO of, and Creative Director for, publishing company Conviction 2 Change LLC. Just Duléa received her B.B.A. in Business Law and Accounting from the University of Miami and is pursuing her M.F.A. in Creative Writing (poetry) from San Francisco State University. Her other titles include, *What Really Happened to Cyrano: The Untold Story of Cyrano de Bergerac (2015), A Poetic Expression of Change (2015), and S.W.A.G. – Saved With Amazing Grace (2016).* Just Duléa is currently residing in San Francisco, CA.

www.ingramcontent.com/pod-product-compliance
Lightning Source LLC
Chambersburg PA
CBHW022115090426
42743CB00008B/856